07-BZK-842

ESP

BY LISA OWINGS

BELLWETHER MEDIA • MINNEAPOLIS, MN

EPIC BOOKS are no ordinary books. They burst with intense action, high-speed heroics, and shadows of the unknown. Are you ready for an Epic adventure?

This edition first published in 2015 by Bellwether Media, Inc.

No part of this publication may be reproduced in whole or in part without written permission of the publisher. For information regarding permission, write to Bellwether Media, Inc., Attention: Permissions Department, 5357 Penn Avenue South, Minneapolis, MN 55419.

Library of Congress Cataloging-in-Publication Data

Owings, Lisa.
 ESP / by Lisa Owings.
   pages cm. – (Epic: Unexplained Mysteries)
 Includes bibliographical references and index.
 Summary: "Engaging images accompany information about ESP. The combination of high-interest subject matter and light text is intended for students in grades 2 through 7"– Provided by publisher.
 Audience: Ages 7-12.
 ISBN 978-1-62617-201-2 (hardcover : alk. paper)
 1. Extrasensory perception–Juvenile literature. I. Title.
 BF1321.O95 2015
 133.8–dc23
                         2014034778

Designed by Jon Eppard.

Printed in the United States of America, North Mankato, MN.

TABLE OF CONTENTS

A BAD FEELING

A young boy opens his eyes. "Ready or not, here I come!" he calls. He runs through the woods where his friends are hiding. Suddenly, panic washes over him. He knows something is wrong.

The boy races deeper into the woods. He finds one of his friends lying hurt on the ground. He yells for help. But how did he know his friend was in trouble?

EXTRA SENSES

ESP stands for **extrasensory perception**. People have long claimed to have this "sixth sense." They know things without using one of the five senses.

THE OTHER SIDE

Some people with ESP believe they can talk with spirits. They try to help people connect with lost loved ones.

There are three main types of ESP. **Telepathy** is reading someone's thoughts. Someone with **precognition** can see the future. **Clairvoyance** is knowing about something happening far away.

THE TWIN CONNECTION

Twins often claim to experience telepathy. Some can finish each other's sentences. Others feel when their twin is in pain.

Scientists have studied ESP since the 1800s. They use cards and photos to test for it. But so far, science cannot prove or deny ESP.

Scientist Karl Zener made cards for ESP studies. They had five simple shapes. One person tried to send a shape by thought. Another tried to guess which shape it was.

IS ESP REAL?

Believers in ESP often claim to have experienced it. Some have suddenly known a loved one was in danger. Others have had **visions** that later came true.

15

Some studies show ESP may be real. On tests, **psychics** often do slightly better than if they were guessing.

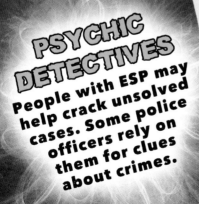

Skeptics believe ESP is **coincidence**. Close friends only seem to read one another's thoughts. If **predictions** come true, it is by chance.

TYPES OF ESP

CLAIRVOYANCE:
Knowing things without experiencing them or hearing about them

PRECOGNITION:
Sensing what will happen in the future

PSYCHOMETRY:
Receiving knowledge or visions by touching an object

RETROCOGNITION:
Sensing what happened in the distant past

TELEPATHY:
Reading others' thoughts or emotions

No one knows for sure whether ESP is real. But most of us have moments that make us wonder. Is it all just chance? Or should we open our minds to ESP?

GLOSSARY

clairvoyance—knowing about distant people, places, objects, or events

coincidence—when things agree or happen at the same time by chance

extrasensory perception—knowing things without using the five senses

precognition—seeing the future

predictions—thoughts or statements about what will happen in the future

psychics—people who claim to have ESP or other unexplained abilities

skeptics—people who doubt the truth of something

telepathy—sensing others' thoughts or feelings

visions—things seen that could be real or imagined

TO LEARN MORE

At the Library

Doeden, Matt. *Nostradamus*. Mankato, Minn.: Capstone Press, 2007.

Higgins, Nadia. *Ghosts*. Minneapolis, Minn.: Bellwether Media, 2014.

Perish, Patrick. *Is ESP Real?* Mankato, Minn.: Amicus, 2014.

On the Web

Learning more about ESP is as easy as 1, 2, 3.

1. Go to www.factsurfer.com.

2. Enter "ESP" into the search box.

3. Click the "Surf" button and you will see a list of related web sites.

With factsurfer.com, finding more information is just a click away.

INDEX